"There is, writes the poet, 'a pretty loud party going on in the other world.' And with those words David Craig takes us on a journey of spiritual longing where 'each little moment' on earth, though suffused with astonishment and love, is only a 'pauper's map to heaven.' Throughout this book, the reader encounters the quotidian juxtaposed with the extraordinary—each and all a wonder. While Craig tells us, we might be 'more lost/than would seem possible,' he also exquisitely reminds us that 'It takes nothing/to truly celebrate.'"

—LOIS ROMA-DEELEY, author of *The Short List of Certainties*

"David Craig's poems read like something written by a hip Franciscan, filled with a surprising sense of self-effacement and humility, mixed with a continual note of celebration for the things of this world: sunsets, sunrises, the chirp of birds, his beautiful family, the happy howl of his two dogs. Somehow he makes you feel, as he says, as if Jesus were in fact, 'to walk down the middle of our street / happy to sit with us on our back porch,' to 'talk about whatever we need to belong to / at the moment.'"

—PAUL MARIANI, author of *Epitaphs for the Journey*

"David Craig is one of the best poets working today. His poetic vision might be best described as 'mystical realism,' and to serve that vision, Craig has evolved a demotic yet lyric style that resembles Emily Dickinson's in its nerve-end economy, William Carlos Williams's in its plainspoken diction and disarmingly unpretentious tropes, and CK Williams's in its candor of address."

—DAVID IMPASTATO, editor of *Upholding Mystery*

"The speaker of this collection is someone the reader wants to visit with and learn from. The subtle fusion of tenor and vehicle in his metaphors is a good technique for a fine Catholic poet whose readers need not be Catholic, but only seekers after the metaphysical, trying to find a refreshed vision. On one level these are simply poems about innocence and grace, and how these factors serve as a compass for living a good life in a society where they are underrated and ignored. This collection is satisfying to mind, heart, and spirit. The reader will return to it for refreshment and inspiration."

—JANET MCCANN, author of *Buddha in the Barbed-Wire Garden*

"I believe David Craig to be the foremost religious poet of the day whose special gift it is to reveal the presence and care of God in all things—especially the most unlikely things. He gives us poems as rich in humanity as they are of the mystery of God, which is the same. He is doing the work he was called for, and we are blessed by the presence his words generate."

—HOWARD MCCORD, author of *Collected Poems*

"This collection is clear-minded, heartfelt, and so reverent it seems irreverent. 'That is why I beat this drum, walking up and down the property line.' Honest and giddy, grateful and 'I don't know, happy,' all the reader can do is rejoice over the fact that there is this kind of voice; that is if he or she doesn't mind sharing the trolley with Barbie and Ken, a horde of slothful tortoises."

—PERIWINKLE BLEU, Bon Vivant, Wife-About-Town

Jesus

Jesus

poems

BY
DAVID CRAIG

RESOURCE *Publications* • Eugene, Oregon

JESUS
poems

Resource Publications
An Imprint of Wipf and Stock Publishers
199 W. 8th Ave., Suite 3
Eugene, OR 97401

www.wipfandstock.com

PAPERBACK ISBN: 978-1-5326-4688-1
HARDCOVER ISBN: 978-1-5326-4689-8
EBOOK ISBN: 978-1-5326-4690-4

Manufactured in the U.S.A.

Contents

I.

THIN 19TH CENTURY GRAVESTONES

are best, how they lean forward, back,
though newer, thicker, those more deeply-etched
dip off-center (sideways) as well, perhaps weighing
their lucre. In either case, there seems to be
a pretty loud party going on in the other world:
maybe the late-night housekeeping staff?
Plastic cups left everywhere, one or two on a marker.
But how and to whom can you complain?

They've left parents to be there, old phone numbers,
baseball mitts—giving up the sunny world
for the sun; though it seems bad manners,
not to keep the directly-behind in order.
And what do the rest of us get out of this disarray:
morning's cut of springtime, greenest grass?

It's enough to turn you into Rodin, a thinker,
a college sophomore.

The sun will set again this evening. I may not like it,
but it will—in its going. (Nobody ever asks me
what I think about anything!)
More last birds, and soon enough the night
will breathe its dark and pleasant way in, get
all mythic, talking to us about the great space
between stars, Steven Hawking.

Here, on this side, all parties fail—as every
Buddhist knows, either for want of success
or because the joy cannot last, or come again. All
that's left for us is giving: a consolation, as we ghost—
never complete–our sunny days, ordering dust,
furniture, waiting for the rest of us to show up.

IT'S HOLY SATURDAY

again, and what could exist, does—
but not here. It's spring
as it doesn't happen in West Virginia:
humps of green daffodils, trees,
their darkened daylight dress.

His smile does not fill these skies;
our lives, a sigh: a wait
for what we would be.

And so this is where we work—
a shop for shavings or bits of stone;
an apron, all the little Geppettos,
Gaudier-Brzeskas; each, every day,
to his scappy corner, finding
drama, inventing epics.

Days need filling—stars invent the sky.
At least that's what we tell ourselves:
rose petals covering the sidewalk,
a heart taking its sleeve.

And what else but resurrection
could give this? We speak words
that own us, dance to the we they make.
We are like torn flags high above
this heading, our do-wops, the tongues
of angels and flying fish.

Come into the shop sometime.
We will find the beer.

THE DOG HOWLS WHEN LINDA PLAYS PIANO

gets nocturnal—lunar white depressions,
vast, dim seas. He feels the ocean in dark leaves,
laments for us all—a world that eats its own.
It's his burden, to bring what his masters can't:
life, a gut-bag on the forest floor, downy drifts
rocking tall limbs, reasons for distress.

I wouldn't want to live there, greased,
though perhaps we do so when we enter the world
of basement laundry. Or maybe we go through
our rounds to keep us from its cold fissures.

My daughter has a burden for the small
of this world, for women. That is why we, parents,
re-spell "grass": ferning colors, building.

There is no security on this frozen dirt, except
in the fact that God brings the world to bear
so heavily upon us—that we, reduced to who
we are, might leave a print, worthy
of the dust and forms we find.

OUR OTHER DOG DIED,
WHICH WAS HARDER FOR HIM

though I suppose it's always like that—
the going one making all the noise.
I'm sure I'll be hac-hec-hooing right along
with Muriel Spark, everyone else
when it's my turn to brave
that cold amusement park.

I wish my ride could be like a saint's,
but it hasn't been. And if there's anybody
doing that down at the college, you
wouldn't know it—which makes sense,
given the noisiness of my coaster car—
quieting the world's not an option.
No, I'm afraid most of us are like the many,
bumbling our way through, too much
of the holy water finding floor
as we enter or leave the church.
We are the great (spiritually) unwashed,
the mass who, we hope, will get into heaven
at a group-rate, kind of like Walmart shoppers.
"Yes, yes," Peter a little bored, waving us
through with our small busy flags.

They'll be a place for us at the bar, too,
in heaven, though many will leave
(not judging of course as we enter).
It will just be so many, too many new
dart games, too much loud talk for them,
too much carrying on—though we might
see Francis somewhere, quiet, grinning.
Everyone except Dodger fans.
(I have no idea why that should be.)

We'd all get quiet for the sunset though,
the huge heavenly ship going down.
Then it will be new stars and night birds,
tennis over to the right, under leaves, lights.
The whole place will be like a cathedral
with posters on the trees.

I STILL LOOK FOR HIM BENEATH THE TABLE

laying there, spent, when I tuck:
the little general who passed
like bright sails among us.
Dogs are little guardians, aren't they,
signposts, doing their job,
telling you about selflessness again?
Of course they are only dogs,
but that's kind of the point, isn't it?
("Here, friend, the answer's by the biscuit.")

We can use all the help we can get.
That's why we bring them in
in the first place. And they do it all
so single-mindedly. "Yep, yep.
I can do that while I'm biting this."

I suspect they are close to the angels:
everybody gets one of each.
And anyone that faithful gets the run
of the land, which is nice recompense,
our backyard, having been so small,
our walks, so few.

"Yes, yes, get off your ass. That's right.
How else will we get where we're going?"

FR. BOB LOOKS SO OLD AT 82

And it's happening to all of us.
We get up each morning
to see what the mirror's been up to,
move through the seas of our flesh—
which ain't too happy about it.

Well, let that be.
They are the world and all of its woes:
neighbors, garbage men, late again.
None of us ever expected this,
the quiet rebellion, one cell at a time.
(And rebels never know
where they are going, do they?
That's part of the charm: trying
to picture an end their new order
can never create.)

Here, though, I saw him on Facebook,
in his rocking chair: birthday, snappy
shirt beneath the sports coat,
Madonna House north woods porch.

Some people shouldn't leave.
It's really that simple.
There should be, instead, a field
of statues: folks just like them,
all life-sized, not on pedestals,
but in the middle, moderate to high grass,
flowers there, their favorite books, pencils—
no sign telling you how to get there!

I don't want to go,
but you can count me as a breath
who came after.

AND IF AT TIMES I FEEL LIKE PIGPEN

at the University, my rising dust cloud,
charming—because contained;
as if I've become a kind of local color
in the halls, a man who might be seen,
talking to himself on a corner
of the stage, next to Schroeder
who is almost listening, at his piano;
Lucy, finally dancing—at the climax
of the Christmas show, I know too
that I have somewhere to go
when this night is over, the last
trace of carolers, lingering
in the animated air:

to the crib, (Schroeder's music
again, now distant, soft) where dirt,
airborne debris are not new or
unexpected, where the ones who do
not fit, do—along with hedges, possum
faces, king's men. So let these others
speak their hard truths about me.

"It is so. It is so."
No self-respecting institution
would have me. I do not fit in—perhaps
because I am what they will not see
about themselves, though
I could not insist on that.

SUMMER LOOMS, A VERY BIG PEONY

bobbing its head: Huck Finn with a hall pass,
corridors, big as all outdoors. Expansiveness
is your middle name, your hum, the only
music you need down this path.

Summer is who you roll with:
my wife in a canoe, a short son—
the bane of Iceland.

It's good we have no need for skata, its smell.
(Would they prepare it carefully
if it had an extra chromosome?)

Love is a chubby Down's hand;
Jude, our grumpy angel, like the summer
where this poem was going—
a generous place with little in the way
of expectation, besides "fun" (us,
dunking that boat our first time out).

The world curses itself, becomes cold,
Icelandic in its monstrous ego.

The answer has always been in another place,
small and green enough for a person
to rejoice in his ability just to run
on asphalt, arms and legs, compact pistons,
his slightly ample gut in the rearview mirror,
showing you just how much you are worth.

LET ME PICK MY BERRIES HERE

in stone shoes, an idyllic embarrassment;
left-handed, we are Mm. Gauches,
Studebakers—odd at every possible turn.

Southpaw prophets, we are old
spinning drive shafts, universal joints:
products of a sinister ingenuity; goat-like,
the roundabout way we get us done.

A room of flakes, we are noisy with
invention. No one can predict our lefts
(Christ's rights).

The world is a hydraulic wrench,
a pounded socket: a whole lot of noise
and disappointment—outside the shop,
which does not own us either.

God is left-handed, invented Louis Pasteur.

Does He proceed in expected ways?
Surely not. He has stopped the sun
upon occasion, chooses only
those whom He likes, which in this
odd case, happens to be you
(and probably most of your friends).

SELF-REFLEXIVE IN THE PARKING LOT

I turn my folding chair in another
direction, grind the legs to stabilize.

Who will show up next?
(How will they get here?)
And why the bone-white sky?

A corrugated aluminum building
squats on one side, a parking lot,
an open field stretches the other.

I wonder, what does this mean?

I stand on the chair,
not for speech or vantage, but to
make a personal statement.
First on one foot, bending, arms out
for flight. Later, spinning the chair
on one leg, I want to call it strumpet
for leaving me alone,
without care or resources.
And then, finally, as night comes:
"You win. . . . Liar."

Had I matches I would light
a fire, offer tomorrow to the moon,
a pile of worn tires.

I may get weary here, but I'm not
going anywhere. And if I have to,
I'll carry it on my head.

Life is what it is, you know that,
but so are you.

THE MONKS HAVE IT RIGHT

Stop, get out and stand
next to the yellow tortoise
on the blisteringly hot county road.
(It's in the *Philokalia*.)

You wonder about the Paleolithic color?
Danger? Maybe it's the intense heat,
the wavering soft asphalt sear
that makes that happen.

Later, driving back, its head
raised, now in attack mode—
a small god on the first road.

Is this St. Paul's thorn,
blank answer, the one he couldn't get?
The sufficient grace, a canvas?
My Down's son and I move on,
stop later at a store, buy pops.

What is it I'm showing him?
That this is what you start with,
or that this is where we end?
A world we can only see.

(The car door makes its curiously
complex sound when I open it:
the product, expression
of the entire industrial revolution.)

Wherever we go today, we walk
a scorched field, bare-faced. The bees
and butterflies might distract us,
but only for a while. Heat soon begins
to oppress, weigh us down; our clothes
become hot, too heavy. We lose an inch—
which is a lot harder for him.

ALL THE HELP WE NEED

It isn't exactly a friendly infection
that crawls us to daily Mass, that pews us
next to the other spindled wolves,
our grim insistences. (Our suits don't quite
fit, as we lick a paw, scratching on the sly.)

The whole thing is beyond us. I mean,
who could imagine God lifting your snout—
signing you up for the parish volleyball team?

We turn, grateful, but never completely,
small-time Richard the Thirds in face paint,
scarce half made up; we feel stuck
above our sinks, with an extra hand, ear.

We don't know how to wash up, or who
to listen to. This is best. We all know that,
a truth that reveals itself, missing. I come up
short again in my classes, scratching.

Whatever we can manage, it's not enough:
the half note we howl, slopping around
the gene pool like some 50s Swamp Thing.
And the world has never been particularly
helpful either, on Facebook
or in our more nurtured successes.

Kicking dirt, we try to bless everyone,
even as our parents occasionally break in—
only to ease back, under graveyard sod.

THE WIND IN WAVES, UP THE HIGH GRASSY HILL

like a thousand soldiers in rural, genial rise.
The occasional sunny tree along the country
road, too, pleases in full dress. What am I
doing driving here? To witness this? I do.

Blue basket, a farmhouse behind us now.
What did we do to deserve this day?

Heck, we've got two dogs, a rice cooker
for God's sake, strawberries in the ground—
my tanned feet inside sandals.
Even now, writing this, when it's evening,
a few birds chirp their song, dogs too
in the distance—the sky doing sunset.

Now is the answer you never asked for.
It would feel like this if Jesus
were to walk down the middle of our street,
happy to sit with Linda and me on our back porch,
talk about whatever we need to belong to
at the moment. Or maybe He'd initiate,
talk about how the best spots get formed
on peaches, or about how conversations
change once you add a fourth voice.

LET ME FIT NOWHERE

Dark trees, their bark in rain,
the rough feel of those places.
I want my fingers to web,
speak another language.

Let me sit under a tree,
a wet toadstool: dripping,
abstracted; let me lose myself in slugs,
slick foliage, creeping.

Waiting is village enough.

Beads of water, serrated grass,
the movement of recovering ants.
They could march across my soul, skull,
open crevices, newly affected areas—
a thousand little feet, no room
for any of them.

DRIVING THROUGH AN AMISH THUNDERSTORM

so many frogs in my lights,
I have to lower my expectations.

What plague is this?

I can't be sure, but I don't want to wake up
some morning, straw-hatted, working
a sweaty fly-bitten hay-field, behind a horse,
speaking botched German. I don't want
to brush it down later,
get intimate during oats.

I'd like my apocalypse to involve better,
more user-friendly computing; Ma Bell
could make a comeback.
I'd like to hear my name
in the sounds of a nearby creek.

Beer at the center of town.

My kids could come back and visit
whenever they felt like it, three generation
in tow. Nobody'd have to say Jesus,
though we could if we wanted.

Old dogs would learn new tricks.
Sainthood would come easy as a pie
on a ledge. Wouldn't be no video games
about cars thieves neither. You could read
a book of poetry, get the kind of breeze
you want—until someone
needs help in raising a barn or
in making one of those little hats.

I GENERALLY RIDE THE GIANT TORTOISE

sloth: modest scepter, bowing,
almost at ease, with the rest of the tardy.
("Woe, woe," I might say, irony
at my wet eye, a slow, bumpy ride.)

The thing will not hurry.

I chase Anthony, Francis,
on the slowest of feet, stretch of neck.
Perhaps I will catch them both
getting stuck in the same door (for years).
Maybe Therese, sewing up a storm.

But, as busy Paul says, His grace
is sufficient, which only means
we're not. Let me bless you, throng,
let me give you the love
you haven't known. Chances are,
we'll never get it right.

We will be snatched up
into the sky in all of our stupidity,
a book of poems in one hand,
a diet cherry Pepsi-Cola in the other.

And that will be okay with God;
in fact, it will have been His idea.

THE GREEN TREE NEXT DOOR

dominates the bay window: it's bold,
clean-edged, could be a sign or something—
standing upright for itself,
waving in the breeze; though personally,
I would feel a little embarrassed: waving the flag
of self before others, in front of God, all of creation.

It's like the thing is a flaming sword or something,
of haughty mien: King David on a horse,
at the front of a bannered column.

No marksman could find him, so severe was he,
so unapologetically, righteously himself.
He was made for it, and he knew the truth in that:
giant-killer, red-haired Menelaus, Achilles.
He disdained deserts, lessers, who here, it
must be stated, was everyone else—
though I bet he cracked his knuckles, something
my mother told me never to do.

Still, bravest is brave: alone but not,
God in his righteous voice. Who could contend with that:
a king or an oak on a bright morning, each what
they are meant to be, glints of divine suffrage?

Disdain will not change either.
They do not play games with versions of themselves.
If that great king ever comes this way, troops in tow,
I want to ask him if he'd break off some of that holy
hauteur, maybe offer a canteen of first water.

I wouldn't know myself—would reek, finally, of tribal
sweat, brothers, behind an affable, grizzled red king.

Outside air would be mine, each subsequent place,
too, when necessary. I would clean up around
the river, camp, a fine partner in an only enterprise.

WHO BETTER THAN THE FALLEN

to cry out "Jesus"—who better
to embarrass us, borderline
hypocrites: we try one way,
are better in another.

We're always waving the wrong flag.
No St. Pauls—we are like
something mechanical, thin metal
strips, boyhood Erector Set
perforations, all the screws,
knobs as we wheeze along the shore
of Galilee, calling out, trying
to get or give too much attention.

We would cry "unmake us,"
but we don't need help with that
as we pause in vacant lots,
gathering up one piece or another
of ourselves.

We are alone because we have
made ourselves that way: dissonant
voices crying a wilderness.

"Save us, save us," we cry out, again,
and it does.

WE WALK INTO A DIFFERENT CAVE

and our names no longer fit.
Here is praise, for everything
that didn't happen, for what is better.

A breeze comes in from the cove.

You hang glyphs on a nearby line, enjoy
the sunlit sound of them clacking together:
they could be barnacles or clams,
drying as they sway.

You could set up shop here, open a store,
but this place is metaphor. You know that.
Your loose shirt, six books beside you
tell you as much.

A young one, in a far-off place,
has found a home today. Skies
brighten along the beach:
Magellan with his oranges.

I didn't know fatherhood
contained this: a daughter
walking an alien shore, not a boat in sight.

REFUGEES MUST LEARN WHAT A RADISH IS

find a taste to name it. They must
wait out the claims of shaking fists, fences.

The larger way of things
offers no repose. And so it should be
for us—the spots we had claimed in the world,
after all, did not have our names on them.

This is how we should be:
someone else's fast—

a need that has no home. Whose census
could claim us, after all:
a people without borders—
Jesus bleeding out on a rug?

And so, though our days might be light,
our stars align for a time, we never can.
We belong to the One who did not stay.

YOU CAN FIND BETTER SHEEP

with a better sense of direction.
The lot of us, wandering this way, that,
stuck in the middle of the road,
no grass to chew, more lost
than would seem possible.

Later, heads into the same tree.

We sing on church steps, but no one
lets us in—because we are sheep.
We cry out, try to say that we are
the only face there is. But
no one understands us.

We keep it up, call out that we
are the hands of the poor. But we
don't have them. Jesus, we say, loves
us, not for who we are,
but for who we are.

No one from inside opens the doors.
Maybe they don't have hands either.

YOUR CRY HAS ALWAYS BEEN SMALL

Around night fires, no one
solicits your opinion. (There is a reason
why you look so unprepossessing.)

And, really, what could be better?

You could start a revolution of farmer songs.
Toadstools on the march—the lot of you,
locking elbows like early Communists.

No one will listen,
but when has that ever stopped you?

THE DESERTED PART OF THE CITY

late night, a young man walking
quickly, hands in his pockets, each street sign
giving him a new name. He is looking
for a future—one that won't steal who he is.

That was a long time ago.

Jesus didn't talk, not on that night.
He sat down—somewhere—among
the graces of falling leaves; easy,
because of the robe, perhaps waiting
for the last constellation to align.

His words, I didn't know then, are always
quiet, give back the clear edges of things,
the way the word "fractal" delivers "leaves."

He is Eliot's tiger, the single note,
the hone and beacon.

He shakes the night out of his robe.

I don't have to be anyone else
on this fine night (either)—waiting for
Moses, Elijah, Diane di Prima.

He is the hole in my every stillness.

PENTECOST COMES BUT ONCE A YEAR
—for Robert Lowell

I plant five crimson paper flames inside
the crib, scour Walmart for red bulbs.

Pentecost, my tree—I crown
with Russia's red dove. Seraph cut-outs
come last, glitter carefully scattered,
Jackson Pollack-style, on each wing.

Later, I watch them waver
in the air-conditioning.

Finally I set some of the straw on fire.
Nothing changes. And so here I am,
in my ash, again, backwards.

*

Today is ordinary time, St. Boniface's day.
He's in red, too, but it's not the same.

Now it's time for all you never wanted.

So I push the couch bed back under itself,
pound some cheese Doritos, vacuum the creases.
I look out the front window for too long
a time, realize that I will never have a day.
And how will I even get to the promised
land, fingers dipped in orange pollen?

Oh Lord, slough this despond:
fill Michelangelo's Sistine face—
turn me into Zossima, a living fire,
or at least a healthy waft.

Let all the limping praise the Lord—
almost successfully. (He is risen, but
too often lies, still, afternoons
on a dark bed upstairs.)

Some of us lie shaded: our leaves,
prone now on the sidewalk, almost exhausted;
while others endure much more, giving
what they can—photosynthesis.

GOD DELIGHTS

in helping us squeeze
through old shells; the road behind—
an uneven trail of cracked debris:
a personal, and therefore,
beneficial embarrassment.

Each has proven too small a house:
a familiar wet birth, a suck,
a vise that doesn't want to let us go.

You realize, of course, that
your grouse doesn't matter—
to anyone, though you do worry
about those who come after:
barefooted, crunching reversals.

But wait, there's no one else
on this road!

And then you notice, too, as you
obsess behind you, how those piles,
strewn bits have begun to gleam,
iridescent, opalesque in
the early sun, fading morning mist.

(Still no company on the road,
just the almost imagined, distant
parade beyond the trees—
a hoopla, a to-do.)

Here it's just the drying,
the reconfiguring of wet shirts.
You could write a book on
muscle memory—until you're
graced with a saving epiphany:
you see that what you've been
producing, is, in fact,
a kind of courage: each
little moment surpassed, a record,
a pauper's map to heaven.

FINDING WALDO

St. Anthony locks his step behind
Jesus. You couldn't hear the sound
his feet made back then. He moved
like daylight—were your birds, Anthony,
the first birds? And the sopping of rain,
could it portend anything,
since it was already speech?

Where you walked the townspeople
could not follow. (Miracles, like little
dogs, came after.)

You are still like that, fixed behind: no voice
for us, nothing beyond an intimation,
a face on a passing bus. You are the guy
standing next to us. Our job, find you.

WISDOM, LIKE AN OLD HORSE

walks unabated, in circles,
around Joyce, William the Third.
He mills, that's what he does, listening—
doggedly—to what anyone says.

He walks through complaints,
has been called every name in the book—
except Utopia. He's never been called that.

He likes common appellations best:
Joe, Phil, the ones in crew cuts,
the ones who majored in wood shop.
His mother came from family, but those
days are gone. He has dogs, land
for them to run, but no house to speak of.
Who would clean it?

I wish I could help, but my name
got painted on the wrong mailbox;
and now I don't know what to do.
I've sliced the sides of my sneakers in my
haste for speed, hoping that would
lead me home: my stick in the ground.

He adds the horizontal, insists
we sit under no shade, until
my unities scatter, like leaves in the wind.

AND THIS HOUSE, AS I LOOK AT IT

headed for webs and plaster holes
too; even my books—neglected!
What will happen to their pages
when they fall out, meet mice, more
dust, the wooden floor?

On the particular summer morning
I began this, though, it had gotten hot
before the sun had even come up—
the concrete slabs out back, warm, felt
pleasantly rough on my bare feet.

My own—dependencies had begun, again,
as they do today, to rustle in rooms,
their lives calling them—
I don't know what.

As usual, St. Francis was right—
as he could make himself. It takes nothing
to truly celebrate. To be little should be
enough for anyone. We should cultivate
with small hoes, no one noticing
each change of address.

GREEN DAFFODILS, BRAIDED SOON

mowed under. Newer, greener days
skewer the old. It's almost Biblical.

We are voices in a wilderness of front lawns,
which is why we barbeque the birds of summer,
watch for writing in the trees.

The rolled stone never moves a second time:
its remembered sound walks every tumbling leaf
through an unquiet world.

There is nothing here for us yet;
the answers haven't come. And so we invent
an ordinary—flags on our battlements,
horses at dawn, clattering over a draw-bridge,
the sunny later-feel of those fields.

Quietly, on the front stoop, my wife and I
can sit together, wait for the paperboy.
We sometimes lean back, close our eyes,
just to take in the sounds.

WHERE YOU LIVE, YOU DON'T

What you believe in is far away.
He owns you, but it's a lend-lease thing.
He shows up when He needs to, wrote
you a letter once, put it in your spokes.

On some days, you just sit here,
waiting to be someone else—
that, coming more slowly than you'd like.

But will the world wait for you,
preserve a fine felt hat, a sword?

On the other hand, you don't have
to invite them. A small get-together
would be pleasant, some wildflowers
on the table, a family wine.

Everyone you knew on earth
will remember you, all the good parts.
You will be able to live any way you want,
take in a ballgame as if for the first time.
You can take a walk in an early garden
with your wife, grandchildren fading
in and out of view. Your friends
will see you as you truly are.
The timing of it all will have been His,
of course, big enough in scope
to account for all the turns
you had to make before you could be sure.

POPES, POLAND, AND PRESIDENTS

Footprints in the white heart of God,
and the One who directs bullets
actually listens to you!

I walk barefoot on frozen glass,
the cold, moving me inside myself,
one I do not know.

Thankfully, we are not responsible
for much. We go home to a room
with four walls, our breathing.

If we could just turn one page correctly.

But God says: "Sing, Caedmon!
The night is clear. Stars, like all of heaven,
lean down, attentive; it could be your crib.
Angels, even now, lift their hems to
celebrate; look, they foot it in high snow!
What are you waiting for?
The world isn't finished yet."

"Yes, it is," you sigh. It's like
a beautiful white flower, on a stem you
can wave around in snowfall.
It's a cold, golden clasp, an answer
that doesn't realize more than itself.

Later that night, you set out your clock,
tomorrow's clothes.

THE FUTURE IS ALWAYS TOO BIG

That's why we make up so many of them.
I think of my daughter at college—
nothing leading her anywhere she knows.

Older, we have seen our share, none
of them anything more than a shift of smoke.

All I can offer her are the things
that keep me going: my wife, children—.
One day she will stop breathing, this
early shade—of green.

We are all summery vapors, barely here.

May she find this out on her own,
the pick-ax of her choice, there, close by
for the digging. May she find what matters
to her, a seat next to the vein.

OUR MINIATURE SCHNAUZER, FIFTEEN

can barely see, urgently whines, chasing
elusive biscuits along the kitchen linoleum.
(It's hard not to admire him.)

He struggles on that slick surface
to keep from splaying as he sits, from falling
when he walks.

And patience is difficult—since the returns
diminish. (The good seldom comes
with a smile.) You have to bend low
to scruff his ears, coo words
he cannot altogether hear.

Grandpa Paul in Florida makes the situation
human. A large, capable man, he can't
remember his daughter—all his life, now
someone else's memory. We are losing him:
one more singular journey, unlike any other;
losing his harmonica, his fire chief
compassion, composure. It seems odd
to say it this way—but, I liked him—
have—though that impulse denies him
the rest of his journey, which, long after
we're gone, will bring his ship into port.

He will be completed, like everyone else
in heaven, equals: St. Therese and
Gandhi, the lady who's lived here forever
across the street. Grandpa will be a man
none of us had fully known, or could adequately
praise—until that last petal springs open.

MY LAUGHTER MAKES THE TREE WHOLE

We shake together in polo shirts,
watch some backyard tv,
just the two of us, marmalade toast.

Yard work keeps one involved:
weeding, whacking—the earned beer.

We can sit here until the sun sets.
Birds sing, as they have from the beginning.
My name might be Abraham, alone with God
on the plains of Moab. We talk again,
about His laws, football.

That is why I beat this drum,
walking up and down the property line.

If this is how it must be, this is how
it must be. "The King will come, no matter
what anybody says."

II.

THE FOG OUTSIDE THIS MORNING DID NOT COME

on little cat feet. In fact, it had no feet at all.
(How would the construction workers
in the courtyard below take that?)
Of course, you can see what the poets were after,
how gingerly it moves in—on.
The Old Testament proclaims it God's presence:
like that January day we married, slowly,
into marriage. Our favorite prof, no doubt,
feeling alien to the immediate proceedings—
though not, I'm sure, to what would follow:
a generous woman, bearing her man as much
as her children, he carrying her up switchbacks.

We do it all badly, of course.

Great God, do not forget us who have righted
so few wrongs. We forget how doors work,
set the sprinkler out in snow. What we get right
is tentative, what we get wrong
offers a strange consolation.

"You are the King. You are the King."
(We say this all the time.)

It's not enough to change us—so far—as we stir
our cocoa, watch butter melt on toast.
You are what we know. Help us to walk
the straight line. Let that other guy, the drunk,
the man with matted hair, old, old pants,
sleep it off in the barn.

"MY CHANCE FOR COMPLETELY CLEAR SKIN"

the tv tells me. I'm glad I tuned in
(here in the eye doctor's waiting room).
I might not have known.
The world is generous like this, always
willing to lend a hand. It warms one
as we move toward Christmas.
I'll delight in all the town square bulbs,
even believe I have changed—
for a minute or two, or maybe that I can,
which would make a lot of people
close to me happy. My kids
would get me better presents,
my wife might bake me a cake.

But then the weather channel comes on:
other locations, each with a beautiful
skyline. I could move and things
would be completely different.
I could have more generous friends,
ones who would buy me stuff,
a line of products. My books
would sell like hotcakes.

Everybody is so healthy on commercials,
as we might be in our best days.
But then again, I never get to meet people
like that, each so at ease, on the beam.
I'm sure I wouldn't pass muster either,
for which I am immensely grateful.

We get away with who we are in public,
don't we? It's a good thing
nobody ever sees us.

Unless of course they do, and we just
don't register, which I suspect is more true.
That's why we say "hi" in the elevator:
my weirdness to yours, a big family
we would introduce to no one.

PRAISE GOD FOR THIS FLAT, COLD WINTER SKY

my breath over Sheets: doughnut, a hot chocolate.
It was on a morning like this when soldiers crowned Jesus.
But I will skate through much of this one,
almost as if that never happened.

The lions here are Christians, real ones,
the ones who indict us with their love.

Maybe the dead skin of our lives is all we have to give.
Maybe the stars will descend, settle on our shoulders tonight
like pixie dust as we walk through the snow, not too cold—
another fiction, sweet enough to contain
an us we'd like to be.

I waste the time I've been given,
not fruitfully like James Wright on his hammock
at William Duffy's farm, but in my steps which might as well
be somebody else's: my small sacrifices, an accordion
or the monkey. I would do something great for the Lord,
but the pencils I've gathered get away, fall down.

Who would not welcome purgatory,
the chance to gather for a goal made clear each icy morning?

Let the One who leads take ownership here,
let Him reheat the chocolate, though of course, to put
everything on Him would be to bail.

No, we march to our end, carrying it as we go.

I NEED MORE MONEY TO LIVE IN THIS ECONOMY

so please buy this poem. It comes
with a lens of your own. Its value will increase
as years pass: like vintage Kens and Barbies,
sitting in the sun, though it's hard
to make out what any of them are thinking.
Barbara has a pink car, diversity specific, a portrait
of Eddie Murphy dangling on the mirror.
They are with-it, as the kids say, would set the tone
anywhere. You could prop them up
on your coffee table, in off-handed display,
Barbie with a small book in her hand, this one,
sunglasses perched on top of her head,
a ripped Vassar shirt. You could set them up
in front of a cardboard Catholic academy.
He'd have a small crucifix around his neck,
a burka in the back seat—with *The Bell Jar*
and a judge for the Christian Coalition Prize,
in sheer babushka, winged sunglasses,
along for the ride as well, gazing abstractly,
artistically, out a half-opened back window.

Or maybe the two of them could be seated in front
of a gothic cathedral, old town Freiburg.
Barb could be a hep Franciscan nun, at ease, Ken,
homeless, clutching a Pope Francis doll.

In either case, you'd have a conversation starter.
You could invite literary friends over, the kind
you want to make. The whole set-up could be
one of those you-are-defined-by-how-you-respond-
to-this-art pieces: it would be cutting edge.

Your life would never be the same.
People everywhere would know you, escort you
through the fun parts of their cities.
You could be a poet for the ages, would speak
and the landscape would listen, birds would know
your name. In fact, it would be hard to go on—
so much going right. But good poems do that,
don't they, set you up in a room of plenty, roses on
every table, a gold script plaque above every lintel,
your name on it, the sound of a projector as you
enter the room? Things will be as they
should again; you'll feel, I don't know, happy,
as you move about, secure in what comes next.

LET'S HAVE CHRISTMAS AGAIN THIS YEAR

We'll do a tree thing, send out cards
like they do on Valentine's Day.
We can trim it with little wooden birds,
develop eggnog to fit the occasion.
And we'll need someone to deliver the presents,
make it kid-friendly. It will appear in poems
everywhere, the divine Child in a trough.
We can take the day off work. I mean,
what good is culture without these things,
even if we have to make them up.
Poets could sing in clear-throated ease,
praising the birth of the Lamb. (The name of
Jesus will ring in the squares.) There would be
festivals just for that. It could get crazy;
we could spread cheer, hang crosses on
each other's necks as we pass in the streets.

But then I come back to the Christian
book of poems on my lap.

Still, it's nice to stand by the window,
watch the soft flakes fall, the quiet take over,
despite kids yelling on adjacent streets.
They will find their joy, as kids always do.
It's we who need them: they know
how to live here—in cold coats, celebrating
the season we, patiently, wait in.

I DO WANT TO IMPROVE

1.

Wasn't something supposed to happen to us;
weren't we supposed to be made new like wet asparagus
under supermarket rain?

I've worked a good half my life, trying to make up
for my slow start. And there are a bunch of us, too, maybe
a million and a half who can't find their other shoe.
Pray for me, reader, though I bet, if you do
you need that yourself.

We are the delayed, who hardly know time.
We move more slowly than our bodies do, have to catch up
whenever we turn. (We say hello long after you've gone.)

So be patient with us.

2.

Did I tell you I can whistle like a small bird?

No foot like mine has ever trod this earth!
So let's forward as fast as we can. I might catch or wait
for you, all our steps, tortoises', their earnest
moments, their dry, barking throats.

THE VIRGIN MARY, QUEEN OF ALL THE EARTH

and sky, is my friend. Her clothes,
because they are royal, make so much noise
when she moves, she could be a small city—
all those little voices, narratives!

She brings laughter to its home.

Having mothered the first outcast, she knows
how to make a home where we can stand—
takes the fast train to nowhere.
She likes to walk in soft New Mexican rain;
her kitchen door opens outward.

This is where small blooms
hover in her high, patient hands,
each a green sigh above the earth.
She is the woman at the end of the line,
the one who tends the last fire.
(You can hear her breaking kindling in the dark.)

You could start a new race with her—
were that necessary. She smokes a cigarette
every dawn, just to empathize.

Queen of those heavenly courts, a cry
goes up every time she moves—
and really, what else could I ask for?
That she is says enough.

Mary, would You teach me how to move,
how to disappear—in a crash course:
like the waterfalls of creation?

THIS "VEIL" OF TEARS

It's thin mists of rain, delicate ribbons,
one after another, washing our faces
clean as stone—

the whole place, dampened, green,
imbued with death and sin—
as small droplets cover roses.

ANOTHER MAN SINGING IN THE PARK

People pass. Some perhaps like the song,
no one gathers. (If a tree fell there, would
anyone hear?) And so it has always been.
Besides, what matters is the singing.
A little girl understands. She peddles
around him on training wheels,
then goes home, humming her own tune.

Snow falls. The man is still there.
What can be done: this is who he is.
(You might use him as a coat rack,
an apprenticed tree in your doorway.)

He could stand still next to the bookcase,
as silent as all of them, as God.

If you know His way you are not on it.
If you direct traffic you have lost your course.

This is how children proceed: they hurry
to the next thing, unless there is no hurry.
You can hear them across the lawn
any evening, summer or winter, even alone.

It's the world that has gone wrong,
that pours its molten slag into hole after hole.

What else should he be doing?

WE WANT THE KING'S FIREWORKS

pistolas for everyone. We want to skirt
the new edges we cut at a party;
then evening, how it will slowly
die into itself, marble courtyards, the cool
at the end of the day.

We could be friends there, behind the manse,
no belongings dear to us, ice in our glasses.

We could go inside.

It would be time for classical guitar,
though I do not play. It would be good whiskey,
literary conversation, the dogs.

Can there be too much peace?

Which is why we need the sound of metal plates,
the long bar bouncing on the padded floor,
the squeaking of twenty basketball shoes,
my Down's son and me, no plan in the offing.

Life is an egg, an ovoid I cannot crack
or rise above. It's the ceiling in this room.
We try to settle below the occasional falling chip,
but to no avail. It's only plaster;
our lives, the ones we can't shake.

We can raise up dust, feathers,
but all we get is the necessary irritation
of too much time, too little space at our disposal.

We count for so much less than we had supposed!
And what could be healthier than that?

LITTLE TRAINS AT CHRISTMAS, LITTLE GUNS

that sparked, an army helmet,
(our stockings each held a huge navel orange,
a thick peppermint stick).

They tell me those days are gone,
John Wayne with them.
Now it's all agenda, new heresies.

Will they kill us when their time comes?

That's pretty far from Christmas—or not:
the stench, animal movement, hoary mouths,
a surrender always. Herod owns the horizon.

"Good has no home here," the world
still tells us. "Check its address."

But we've never bought that, the bravado,
a fictional ice palace of lies.
It talks to itself, offers only that.

We will wait. There's only one way
to walk Christmas night: ahead, into the cold.

FROST CRUMPLES THE PUMPKIN

like our faces when the Chinese Palace
forgets an egg roll.

But that is not why I'm here;
I'm here to, barefooted, pipe the valley's glee—
though I should add that our particular vale
is laced with icy ribbons of coiled steel,
rusted pale green physical plants which have had
both Japanese and Argentinian names.

Still, count me among the shouters
on snowy nights. The ho-ho-ers—as falling
flakes muffle the sounds on our street.
Count me, too, among the choir on cinders,
those who dance under highest guttered weeds,
alone or in pairs: singing for rum, glory.

Though you can't see Him,
Jesus walks our new university square,
saying hey to everyone. He's robed in
outdated attire, doesn't care about that.

Yes, yes, harder days have come, will come
again in the rust belt, but they are like relatives
you only meet every year at Thanksgiving.

Awkward, but you have to admit there's
a largesse to the proceedings. So you happily
take your self-conscious place every time,
talk when it's your turn, praise the cooks.

That's why the buns are in the oven;
that's why we keep showing up.

THE WORLD IS ENDING,
I READ IT ON THE INTERNET

There are more liars, haters, than truth:
"Type amen if you agree."

Yes, Jesus came to make us whole,
and though I can't say exactly when that will start,
the expectation is something.

So I buy a large cotton candy, walk down
the midway of shattered lives.

Evil, most decidedly, will go; so forgive
the joy, the larks, those who walk, seemingly
unaffected by the screams in this world.

We want to catch up with all our friends
before we meet them, maybe do a two-step
in the aisle of a grocery store.

Jesus draws us all home: the happy, and those
ahead of us, those who drag
half a body over the finish line.

WE ARE NOT THE MOST IMPORTANT ANYTHING

Though, granted, water (or at least the crowd)
should have parted when we entered the room.

We also ran. That's the gist of things.

We pile stones. Go back and get others.
This is the way of freedom. If we are lucky,
they will ask us to sit with them at table
in the next world: on an embarrassingly low chair.
But the conversation will be so easy, the laughter
so sure, no one will remember
where we came from, which is why, I suppose,
we must feel our failures here.

We must live where life is:
each aborted climb, each tumble into truth.
In a heap, at the bottom, that's where love is.

YOU WALK UNDER THE TREES WITHOUT ME

How would I know?
We could be rumors, a box of old baseball cards.
To say I know You I would have to know myself,
the shoreline, the fish. I hear the quiet
I cannot attain, too busy with the crush for attention
which is the world. Perhaps if I had a pocket knife.

I cannot lay claim to anything,
would rather be like Francis, living in, small enough
to be part of the song: the roughage of leaves,
how they move sequentially, like a feather
does, beneath your finger: separation, unity.

I did everything wrong today:
allowed strife when I could have intervened,
and two young people now live closer to their flaws.
The little god has failed again. And it's always
like this: the quiet, waiting, that place
where You are the only answer.
We should be like plants opening.

Would You recognize me?

HOW CAN WE ESCAPE OUR SINS?
WHO WOULD WANT TO?

We are the lost causes, the ones no one sees.
Our world is unknown to them.
Let me live here forever, among the outcasts,
bad haircuts, sawdust, oily jeans.
Let my friends be those who cannot speak well.
Let me be one of the ones He has to pick up,
to settle, make straight. One of the unsure,
whose only Answer keeps saying "Yes."
Let me wonk in torn shoes, on wet streets,
half my shoelaces gone. I don't want to be
with the poets, but with the poor,
those without an answer to give.

How can we trust ourselves?
Every patch is badge to us; every gift, the same!

People who read always seem to read themselves.

How do I lose myself
when I need the fix of every turn?
Let me sit with them, those whom no one asks.
Let me be one who does not count.

JUDE WANTS EVERYONE TO GO TO BED EARLY

Christmas eve. (This is a concern.)
Reindeer, it appears, have good hearing.

Yesterday he shopped, justly, for himself:
a 102 Dalmatians song book.

His prayer list includes Celine Dion,
the voice of Apple Jack.

Every poet should have a Down's child.
It would keep them rooted. Not
that it's bad to sing the west wind, the birds
of the imagination, or to sit on the throne
of politics, though nothing really changes.
(We must shout with the rest.)

But life doesn't truly set in
until you have to grease someone's dry skin,
until he mentions "suffering,"
like he understands the saints
better than you do, until you realize
that you are in over your head.

Our days will lead us through the grave.

ONLY HILLBILLIES GIT TO HEAVEN

You'll need one of them over-the-backhand jugs,
a coverin' hat. Lots of relatives, gap-toothed.
(You got to be healthy among the trees, the squirrels.)
Book learnin' is optional.

Gotta be hand-picked, right off a vine.
Smokey cold berries, hollers, a steel mill
or a railroad trestle nearby. Difficulties
will be hard to come by; moon shine
bright enough to put a tear in your eye.

There's a banjo on every porch, old wood, untreated.
The insides ain't much different: smallish rooms,
a little darker than you might expect.

Just another stepping off place. You could give
yourself another name. It's all part of the same deal.

I had a brother back then, a couple of 'em:
truckers. Potato salad, lots a sun
on the green hills, a hose in summer.
You could count on those things,
and that was okay. Girls came along,
one banging on the front window,
you not fitting in because there was no place to.

It all made a kind of weird sense: baseball,
in the outfield with the birds. It was all heaven.
The long haul. Of course you didn't know
if it wanted anything to do with you.

Turns out it did.

OLD FRIENDS COME BACK (FOR MARK, JOHN)

Crooked voices over the phone!

We hadn't known how to get where we wanted to,
and the trip took longer than we could have imagined—
in so many beaten cars!

God may have the last laugh, but I get some too:
these were people who walked along side me, for years
at a time, through the long row of college trees,
and not, down 55th, to Madden's, Scrooge and Marley's.

I saw them there, heard their every step.

What sweet inventions, these flowers of God,
in taxis, bookstores, near enough beer to sort us through!

Kerouac's "later phases of our lives" ended up being
pretty much the same. The years that took us nowhere
especially new, though I have a beautiful friend, wife,
adult kids, and who'd have thought it possible: a job.

These were the people who made me what good I am.
We loved our youths together, watched them come apart.

Friends, what I could not give back to you then, I do now.
See all the aged saints in heaven, those on earth as well,
dancing their joy on crooked canes!

EGG NOG SPELLS THE SEASON

It has winter in it, its thickness, its happy
dance. Christmas stockings count, too,
if they're up or not. There's something very old
about the proceedings: Nicholas, dropping
money down the chimney. We could be in Turkey.

Children wait around the fires of this night,
always have. It's the night they find reason
for their size, for the sound of clapping mitts
in deep snows. They must hold out,
Peter Pans, against the lies of adulthood.

No change is coming, no world grown rigid
as the buildings downtown. No, they must keep
what they've found, hold Him like a medal
that can swing beneath their shirts.

That is the sound of praise.
That is the corridor that will not go away.

Notes

"Holy Saturday"
Gaudier-Brzeska was a sculptor (and friend) favored by Ezra Pound.

"Our other dog died which was harder for him"
A great story called "Portobello Road," written by Muriel Spark, includes a shallow, dead, unpurged protagonist who uses the phrase "hac-hec-hooing."

"And if at times I feel like Pigpen"
All the characters here, except the narrator, can be found in "Charlie Brown's Christmas Carol," an animated Charles Schultz tv movie.

"Summer looms, a very big peony"
Iceland, over the summer during which time this poem was composed, proudly announced that they had largely rid their lands of Down's Syndrome—by which they meant they had simply killed all of those babies.

"Let me pick my berries here"
"Gauche" and "sinister" are both foreign words for left-handed people. As a young man, intent on a career in baseball, I'd also grown used to the tiresome "flakey" epithet: something that apparently nicely sums up the better-handed.

"Driving through a Amish thunderstorm"
There are no cute little Amish hats (that I know about), but there should be.

"Who better than the fallen"
The "gathering fuel" allusion comes from T. S. Eliot.

"The deserted part of the city"

Diane diPrima, author of *The Poetry Deal*, is a first rate Beat poet.

"Finding Waldo"

Was (and still may be) a silly puzzle for little kids. A cluttered page would offer hope and the passing of time in the doctor's office. (He was there somewhere!)

This quote appeared in a University bulletin: "The saints are like the stars. In his providence, Christ conceals them in a hidden place that they may not shine before others when they might wish to do so. Yet they are always ready to exchange the quiet of contemplation for the works of mercy as soon as they perceive in their heart the invitation of Christ."

—St. Anthony of Padua

"Wisdom, like an old horse"

In Joyce's "The Dead," Gabriel tells a story about an old and thoroughly trained Irish horse which walked continually around the statue of William the Third, a man who had helped to brutally suppress that country.

"Popes, Poland, and presidents"

In his book *A Pope and a President*, Paul Kengor—as well as other, ill-remembered sources—outline the miracles which guided bullets and so saved both John Paul II and Ronald Reagan, (as they were being prepared by Our Lady of Fatima to defeat an evil empire).

Caedmon, a celebrator of creation, was, according to legend, England's first poet.

"I need more money to live in this economy"

Eddie Murphy pointed out in the early 70s that Ken was a "Mo": apparently neighborhood jargon for a homosexual. Great line, though it couldn't be said today. (TOY STORY 3 had some fun with the idea.)

"It's a 'veil' of tears"

"Vale" is the traditional spelling here, but the other proved more interesting.

"Jude want everyone to go to bed early"

Ashley Ball is the voice for My Little Pony's Apple Jack (and Rainbow Dash). Jude proudly considers himself a brony.

www.ingramcontent.com/pod-product-compliance
Lightning Source LLC
Chambersburg PA
CBHW060158070426
42447CB00033B/2202